Table

Tired Of Being Hassled for Documentation as
Nurse in a LTC/SNF?
A Straight-To-The-Point Guide From MDS
Coordinators:
What Exactly It Is We Need From Your Medicare
Documentation
PDPM

How many of you are familiar with the MDS
department in the Long Term Care/Skilled Nursing
Facility where you currently work? How many of
you actually know what MDS means? What about
what they do? How many of you don't understand
why documentation is so important? How many of
you often times skip documenting because you
deem it not "that important? How many of you have
found loopholes and ways to get automatically
generated daily charting forms to close with
incorrect or partial information needed?
You? You too? Oh my not you too! Well allow me
as a MDS Nurse to make it all make sense in
hopes that you'll gain a better understanding and
rank timely and accurate documentation as your
second most important task to complete after
patient care.
Your documentation equates to money for the
facility. How and why, you ask?
So many questions and still no answers huh?
Well allow me to break things down for you and the
information provided here will allow you to be the

Prudent Nurse without the hassle in any Long Term Care/Skilled Nursing Facility you step foot in.

MDS mean Minimum Data Set (Coordinator/Nurse)

MDS completes assessments on every Resident using the information that you as a Nurse document for monetary reimbursement for the Facility. (Without MDS the Facility has no money and you work for free)

Your documentation serves as support with painting an accurate picture on the assessment of the Resident that the MDS Department submits to State and Federal. Your documentation is audited to ensure it is correct before or after reimbursement is received. (That means if your Facility was going to go all out for Nurses Week to show their appreciation and then say its not feasible when the week comes, it's because of your poor documentation or no documentation MDS had to submit, received payment for, got audited and had to pay back so now they have no money to celebrate your week. You'll get a .25 cent pen for all of your HARD work!)

This again reiterates the statement

"Documentation=Money"

In this guide we tell you EXACTLY what we need so there is no guessing. Quick, clear and accurate is how your documentation will be if you reference and become familiar with this guide.

Note: These are your Medicare Management guidelines per the Center for Medicaid/Medicare Services (CMS)
Your MDS department may require additional documentation from you as a Nurse because assessments are completed to satisfy Federal and State guidelines which may vary.

Physical/Occupational Therapy

*Describe exactly how the Resident's ADL's are performed and the amount of assistance provided for the following:
****Bed Mobility
****Transferring
****Eats (G-Tubes included)
****Toilet Use (After care included)
Ambulates
Dresses Self
Bathing and Personal Hygiene
Skilled Nursing Intervention(s)
****Indicates Late Loss ADLs which generates money when documented properly

What MDS gets:
Mr. Jones is in his room lying in bed watching tv with no needs or complaints of pain at this time.
V/S P 62 R16 B/P 120/80 T 97.7

What MDS needs:
Mr. Jones was observed in his room lying in a left lateral recumbent position. Mr. Jones was easily aroused and used his ¼ side rail to help lift his head and respond when his name was called. Mr. Jones is independent with transferring when w/c is in reach and setup assistance when not. Mr. Jones can ambulate roughly 10ft with supervision. Mr Jones requires supervision with toileting and 1

4

person limited assistance with dressing, bathing and personal hygiene. Mr. Jones is independent with eating. Mr. Jones complains of leg pains after attempts to walk further than 10ft. Mr. Jones is provided pain routine pain medication before PT/OT and PRN. V/S P62 R16 B/P 120/80 T 97.7

ADL's are described as Independent, Supervision, Limited Assistance, Extensive Assistance, Total Dependent, or Did not occur.

CHARTING MUST BE DONE DAILY

Speech Therapy

*Describe exactly how the Resident makes their needs known and communicate as well as their ability to swallow food/drinks.
*Describe the Skilled Nursing Intervention(s)

What MDS gets:
Ms. Flounder is sitting in the dining room talking with other Residents while awaiting trays to come out. Ms. Flounder has no complaints of pain or discomfort. VS P-62 R-16 B/P-120/80 T-97.7

What MDS needs:
Ms. Flounder is sitting in the dining room talking with other Residents using her dry erase board as she is still recovering from a CVA that affected her right side and speech. When asked if she was experiencing pain or discomfort, she wrote "no". Ms. Flounder was also asked if she felt confident enough to feed herself to which she wrote "yes". Ms. Flounder is still on a soft diet with thickened liquids and requires a 1 person Supervision when eating. VS P-62 R-16 B/P-120/80 T-97.7

CHARTING MUST BE DONE DAILY

IM/IV Medication Administration/IV ABT Therapy

*Describe the medication, reason for use and nursing skills used while administering medication
*Describe the effectiveness or side effects obcorvod
*Describe how the Resident tolerated the administration

What MDS gets:
Ms. Flora is on IV ABT therapy for infection. No complaints of pain. No noted side effects at this time. Will continue to monitor.

What MDS needs:
Ms. Flora is on IV ABT therapy, Ciprofloxacin, q 12hrs for UTI. IV site observed in right arm, no noted irritation or issues. Ms. Flora was observed for 15 mins after initial start of ABT therapy for possible adverse reactions. None noted at this time. Ms. Flora does appear less confused and states the pain in her abdomen is gone. Urine still has a notable odor. Will continue to monitor.

How Resident tolerated the administration can be described as: IV infiltration, pain, phlebitis, fluid volume overload, etc.

Lab result <u>MUST</u> be on file showing details of infection for IV Antibiotic*

CHARTING MUST BE DONE DAILY

Respiratory Therapy/Impaired Respiratory Status

*Describe ACCURATELY from lung aspect breath sounds
(*rales, wheezes, rhonchi*)
*Describe respiratory rhythm, rate and quality
*Describe respiratory treatment effectiveness if provided
(*oxygen, nebulizers, chest pt, respiratory medications, other medications, etc*)
*Describe any changes in LOC, mental status or anxiety.
*Describe the Resident's comfort level as it relates to respiratory status
*Describe incidents of invasive techniques and cautioning
Describe Resident's overall condition as it relates to their respiratory status along with skilled nursing interventions implemented for comfort and overall status of improvement

What MDS gets:
A box initialed on the EMAR showing scheduled respiratory therapy was provided but the Pre and Post page incomplete or not completed at all
OR
Mr. Ables was provided PRN nebulizer treatment for complaints of wheezing without Pre or Post

supportive documentation to show where Mr. Ables started and how much the treatment improved his status.

What MDS needs:
With most facilities now using EMARs, the charting for your Pre and Post respiratory status should be auto generated if the EMAR is set up correctly. *DO NOT USE WORK AROUND TO SKIP THIS AS MDS CANNOT CLAIM THE TREATMENT IF YOU DO THIS! DO NOT LEAVE INCOMPLETE!*
If your EMAR is not set up correctly you would then have to manually type all Pre and Post titles and information
>>DO NOT FORGET TO DOCUMENT TIME SPENT ON TREATMENT<<

CHARTING MUST BE DONE DAILY

Unstable Insulin Dependent Diabetes Mellitus (IDDM)

*Describe how diabetes has a direct effect on the Resident's functional, medical, cognitive and mood/behavior

*Describe skilled nursing interventions used along with the outcome

*Describe any signs or symptoms related to unstable blood sugar levels

*Make note of Physician's order changes related to insulin injections (On EMAR) for diagnosis of diabetes

What MDS gets:
With most facilities now using EMARs which provide initial boxes showing it was given for routine and per sliding scale, location of injection and how many units with no additional information regarding Residents who have unstable diabetes.

What MDS needs:
Mrs. Slater was observed to be more agitated than normal and too weak to get out of bed independently as she normally does. She required 2x extensive assist to get up and she also appeared to have a heavy bladder incontinence episode. When asked why she didn't get up and go

to the restroom as she normally does or use the call light for assistance she stated she was too tired and felt nauseous since coming back from dialysis. Upon checking her blood sugar using the sliding scale on her EMAR it was found that she was having a hypoglycemic (59mg/dl) episode and was immediately provided orange juice and a snack. A follow up was conducted 30 minutes later where Mrs. Slater appeared to be back functioning like normal and sugar levels were back in range (83mg/dl).

Italic text: ***CHARTING MUST BE DONE DAILY***

Surgical Wounds or Open Lesions (doesn't include rashes, ulcers, & cuts)

*Describe the location & nature of wound along with any pain and interventions used to combat pain
*Describe observations and nursing interventions r/t surgical wound healing process
*Describe any drainage and areas of increased warmth or erythema
*Describe response to any treatments ordered
*Once a week (weekly body audit) describe in detail wound healing process and response to treatment

What MDS gets:
Mr. Thomas has a wound that stretches from both inner thighs down to scrotums r/t infection. Mr. Thomas went out to appt. To wound care clinic this a.m. and is not scheduled for wound care again until tomorrow. Mr. Thomas states he is experiencing a little pain and was provided the PRN pain medication on file. No other complaints of discomfort expressed at this time. Will follow up on effectiveness of PRN pain medication.

What MDS needs:

Mr. Thomas has a surgical wound that stretches from both inner thighs down to his scrotum r/t Fournier's gangrene. Mr. Thomas went out to appt. at wound care clinic this morning and per paperwork, a debridement was performed. Mr. Thomas was assessed for pain, for which he stated was present and currently a 5 on a scale of 1-10. PRN pain medication provided. Will follow up for effectiveness. No drainage noted to bandages, no warmth or erythema. Daily wound care provided in house and response to recent debridement will be observed, and noted in detail during weekly body audit scheduled for Wednesday.

Most facilities have in-house wound care nurses but will also send Residents out to wound care clinics depending on the extent of the wound. Wound care nurses usually perform body audits and log the in depth details of the surgical wound healing process (*this is facility specific so do inquire with your facility about protocol*). You will still have to perform weekly body audits as the Nurse for said Resident so become familiar with where to find the Wound Care Nurse's notes as well as how to describe surgical wounds.
CHARTING MUST BE DONE DAILY

New Gastrostomy Tube Feeding

*Describe clinical necessity for G-tube/J-tube
*Describe amount of fluids/feedings delivered
*Describe how tube feeding was tolerated with special attention to adverse effects such as: abdominal distention, diarrhea, abnormal lung sounds or cardiac related symptoms
*Describe type of ostomy care rendered to G-tube site and condition of site

What MDS gets:
With most facilities now using EMARS initial boxes are provided for signature showing feedings were completed and the amount of fluid and food q shift and 24hrs leaving the specifics needed regarding new G-tube required by the Center for Medicaid and Medicare services undocumented.

What MDS needs:
Mrs. Hall showed to have more than a 5% weight loss over the last 30 days. ST

referred for barium swallow which diagnosed esophageal stricture. Mrs. Hall was sent out for G-tube placement per Physician's order and has since returned. Day 1 post placement: Mrs. Hall tolerated her first feeding (Pivot 1.5 with 60cc of water) via g-tube very well. Mrs. Hall was observed for 30 minutes after for adverse effects to which none was noted. Mrs. Hall is set to have ostomy care every 72 hours and PRN per MD orders with cleaning using soap and water and new dressings applied. Current condition shows no drainage, irritation or infection at this time. Mrs. Hall has no pain or discomfort. Wound care nurse made aware of new ostomy.

CHARTING MUST BE DONE DAILY

Straight Catheterization/GU Complications

*Describe nature of condition that warrants use of straight catheterization
*Describe use of sterile techniques during oathoter administration
*Describe any resident teaching
*Describe present clinical conditions that require skilled nursing observation (*indicators of UTI, dysuria, frequency, urinary retention etc*)

What MDS gets:
With most facilities now using EMARs there is a box placed to initial showing catheterization was completed and how much was captured on the TAR which leaves the additional information needed for supportive documentation unavailable.

What MDS needs:
New orders received for Mr. Olge who is a paraplegia with a new diagnosis of BPH and UTI for straight catheterization q 6 hours and PRN. Mr. Olge was explained that the new order received was to help him alleviate himself (urinary retention) which is documented he complained about for over a

week before his diagnosis. He was then explained the procedure and shown the equipment that would be used. Mr. Olge voiced understanding. Sterile techniques were then started and the initial catheterization was completed without issues. 300cc of urine was captured, no blood, odor, or cloudiness noted.

CHARTING MUST BE DONE DAILY

Decubitis Ulceration Stage III or IV or Multi IIs with 2+Skin Treatments

*Provide stage and condition of wound
(*YOU CANNOT BACKSTAGE, EVER*)
*Describe nursing interventions used to prevent further ulcer development
*Describe skilled nursing interventions used to aid in wound healing
*Describe dietary interventions & consumption amounts of meals and fluids provided
*Describe response to current treatment
*Describe overall skin condition
(*bruises, edema, redness, cyanosis, abnormalities, poor skin turgor, rashes, etc*)
*Provide interventions as it r/t abnormal lab values
*Once a week (weekly body audit) describe in detail wound measurements, locations and response to treatment

What MDS gets:
Ms. Johnson has a stage III of the sacrum. Wound care provided by wound care nurse. See *forms for details
OR

Ms. Johnson has a stage III of the sacrum. Wound care provided per TAR, no noted issues, no complaints of pain or discomfort.

What MDS needs:
Ms. Johnson has a stage III wound of the sacrum that was present on admission. Stage III 2 ½ inches wide, 1cm in depth currently has healthy pink tissue with a minuit opening about 2cm wide. Daily wound care provided, Ms. Johnson is turned q 2 hrs and PRN and provided a chair cushion when in w/c for prevention and healing purposes. Ms. Johnson has great skin turgor, ointment is applied to skin during daily ADL care, no rashes, bruises or other areas of skin breakdown noted. Ms. Johnson is on a high protein diet per recommendations of RD and receives Juven 1.5 q shift for supplement. Per MD orders, labs are taken yearly and PRN and observed for abnormal readings. Wound care nurse conducts once a week body audit to capture measurements, location, treatment and response to treatment.

Most facilities have in-house wound care nurses but will also send Residents out to wound care clinics depending on the extent of the wound. Wound care nurses usually perform body audits and log the in depth details of the surgical wound healing process (*this is facility specific so do inquire with your facility about protocol*). You will still have to perform weekly body audits as the

Nurse for said Resident so become familiar with where to find the Wound Care Nurse's notes as well as how to describe surgical wounds.
CHARTING MUST BE DONE DAILY

Cerebral Palsy/Multiple Sclerosis/Quadriplegia/ Hemiplegia

*Describe ADL status as well as skilled nursing interventions used to assist Resident improve ADL deficits

What MDS gets:

Mr. Alexander was observed sitting in his w/c in the day room watching television while having coffee. Mr. Alexander has no complaints of pain or discomfort at this time. VS P-62 R-16 BP-120/80 T-97.7 O2-98RA

What MDS needs:
Mr. Alexander was observed sitting in his w/c in the day room watching television while being supervised by a Nurse Aide as he attempted to lift and hold a coffee mug in his right hand. When Mr. Alexander's name was called, he waved his left hand and began shuffling his feet in an attempt to ambulate himself in his w/c towards the medication cart for vitals. Mr. Alexander is total dependent with

locomotion on the unit and required a 1 person assist to the med cart. Mr. Alexander stated he had no pains or discomfort at this time. VS P-62 R-16 BP-120/80 T-97.7 O2-98RA

CHARTING MUST BE DONE DAILY

Fever

*Describe skilled nursing interventions and observations used to maintain homeostasis (Fever is defined as a temperature 2.4 degrees F higher than baseline. The resident's baseline temperature should be established prior to the Assessment Reference Date)

What MDS gets:
With most facilities now using EMARs a box is provided to initial that the PRN medication on file to be given for fever has been given leaving the supportive documentation needed unavailable.

What MDS needs:
Mr. Hernandez complained of feeling overheated while attending activities. Activities department called for Mr. Hernandez's nurse who noticed he was sweating profusely and immediately inquired about pain and taking vitals. Mr. Hernandez stated he had been having tooth pains since lunch and that he called a dentist on his cell but did not get an answer. VS P-76 R-18 B/P- 138/82 T-100.2 Baseline 97.7. Upon observation it appears Mr. Hernandez had an extensive cavity and notable gum irritation. PRN pain medication (500mg acetaminophen) on file was provided, MD/RP notified. New orders for Percodan 325mg were received per MD orders and Mr. Hernandez has

been scheduled for an appt. tomorrow with his family dentist. Will continue to assess pain/fever and effectiveness of medications q 15mins.

Vomiting

*Describe skilled nursing observations and interventions used to maintain homeostasis

What MDS gets:
Mrs. Harber's nursing assistant reported what appeared to be vomit on the floor beside. Assisted with getting Mrs. Harber cleaned up and provided PRN antiemetics on file. Will continue to monitor.

What MDS needs:
Mrs. Harber's nursing assistant reported what appeared to be vomit on the floor beside. Mrs. Harber stated she had been vomiting since this morning. When asked what all she had eaten today, she stated nothing because she had been feeling nauseous since taking her meds this morning. A review of her morning medication shows she takes vitamin D supplements which per instructions should be taken with food to avoid nausea and vomiting. Mrs. Harber was assessed for pain to which she stated she did not have just nausea. Mrs. Harber was provided PRN Zofran 8mg on file along with food and fluids for rehydration. Interventions proved effective, Mrs. Harber was educated on why it is important for her to eat a bite of breakfast before taking her morning

medication. Mrs. Harber voiced understanding and has no other questions or concerns at this time. VS P-62 R-18 B/P-120/80 T-97.7 02-98% RA

Dehydration

*Describe skilled nursing observations and interventions used to maintain homeostasis

What MDS gets:

Mr. Rale's nursing assistant reported that Mr. Rales keeps spitting on the floor. Mr. Rales was observed and asked why he keeps spitting on the floor. He stated "I don't know, my mouth just keeps telling me to spit and my skin keeps telling me to scratch. I want some water." Mr. Rales was provided water via peg tube and lotion applied to body. No complaints of pain or other discomforts at this time.

What MDS needs:

Mr. Rale's nursing assistance reported that Mr. Rales keeps spitting on the floor. Mr. Rales was observed and asked why he keeps spitting on the floor. He stated "I don't know, my mouth just keeps telling me to spit and my skin keeps telling me to scratch." It is observed that Mr. Rales has a peg tube (with orders for a pleasure tray), cracked lips and broken areas of skin where he has been scratching. Skin turgor showed tented, eyes appear sunken. MD was contacted and sent over orders to have labs taken which showed positive for dehydration. Orders for glycerin treatment of the mouth and lip balm 2x q shift, a 120cc increase in fluids q shift PO with observation for adverse effects, q shift intake and output, and another order for labs were sent over per MD. If no improvements within 24hrs, send out for IV hydration. Will continue to monitor closely.

Internal Bleeding

*Describe skilled nursing observations and interventions used to maintain homeostasis r/t anemia
(fatigue, skin color, signs of shock, ect)

What MDS gets:
Mr. Hobb's Nursing aide reported seeing blood during perineal care this a.m. MD notified and orders were sent over to send out to the hospital for further observation. VS P-62 R-18 B/P 120/80 T-97.7 O2-98% RA

What MDS needs:
Mr. Hobb's Nursing aide reported seeing blood during perineal care 2x this a.m. Mr. Hobbs was observed and assessed for signs of shock, no change in skin color noted and Mr. Hobbs is up and getting dressed with extensive assistance like usual. Pain assessment completed, Mr. Hobbs has no complaints of pain or discomfort. No vomiting reported. MD notified and sent over orders to have Mr. Hobbs sent out for further observation. VS P-62 R-16, B/P-120/80 T-97.7 O2-98% RA

Dialysis

*Describe skilled nursing interventions and observations used to maintain homeostasis

What MDS gets:
Mrs. Rose went out for dialysis today and was seen returning to the building by ambulance service at 13.02 on stretcher.

What MDS needs:
Mrs. Rose went out for dialysis today and was seen returning to the building by ambulance service at 13:02 on stretcher. Mrs. Rose access site shows no bleeding or swelling. Mrs. Rose was provided lunch and p.m. medication. Fluid restrictions are in place, no noted edema, complaints of pain or discomfort. Dialysis sheet/form completed and placed on Mrs. Rose's chart with pre/post vitals. VS P-62 R-18 B/P-120/80 T-97.7 O2-98%

***Always keep a copy of the dialysis sheet sent out with the resident for your reference and to avoid having to create a new document for MDS with not so accurate information

Falls

*Describe post skilled nursing observations and interventions

What MDS gets:

Mr. Howell was found by nurse aide on the floor beside his bed. No injuries noted, no complaints of pain. Administrator and R/P notified. VS P-62 R-18 B/P-120/80 T- 97.7 O2-98% RA

What MDS needs:
Mr. Howell was found by nurse aide on the floor beside his bed. Back against the bed, legs straight out, resting on right arm. Mr. Howell was assessed for injury to which none was noted. Incident report completed, pain assessment completed, neuro checks started per facilities protocol. ROM checked, Mr. Howell is of sound mind and was asked if he felt he needed to have an x-ray done to which he stated no. Further monitoring to determine put in place. When asked how did he fall Mr. Howell stated he was trying to roll over in the bed. Intervention added to careplan (fall mats)and fall risk assessment completed. MD/RP and ***Administrator notified***.

Red highlights are MANDATORY when a fall takes place

Infections
**See *ABT Therapy*

Behaviors

*Describe cognitive and behavioral symptomology:
Cognitive loss and severity
(*orientation to place, person, time and memory
deficits long/short term*)
Signs of depression
(negative statements, calling out, sad/anxious
appearance, self deprecation, withdrawn, etc)
Behavior symptoms
(verbally abusive, socially inappropriate,
resistant to care, wandering the halls and into
other room)
Delusions/Hallucinations

What MDS gets:
NOTHING FROM THE RESIDENT's NURSE!!!!!

What MDS needs:
An accurate description of unusual behavior,
decreasing cognition, signs of depression,
delusions/hallucinations instead of it just being
brushed off and never mentioned.

**Absence of this documentation does affect
scoring which equates to money!

Didn't see what you needed here? Let us know.
We'd like to hear from you!
klknursingstrategies@gmail.com
Or Visit
https://klknursingstrategies.teachable.com

Made in the USA
Columbia, SC
08 August 2024